Addressing Inclusion and Inequalities through PSHE and Citizenship

Simon Blake and Sue Plant

national
children's
bureau

making a difference

National Children's Bureau

NCB promotes the voices, interests and well-being of all children and young people across every aspect of their lives. As an umbrella body for the children's sector in England and Northern Ireland, NCB provides essential information on policy, research and best practice for its members and other partners.

NCB aims to:
- challenge disadvantage in childhood
- work with children and young people to ensure they are involved in all matters that affect their lives
- promote multidisciplinary cross-agency partnerships and good practice
- influence government policy through policy development and advocacy
- undertake high quality research and work from an evidence-based perspective
- disseminate information to all those working with children and young people, and to children and young people themselves.

NCB has adopted and works within the UN Convention on the Rights of the Child.

Published by the National Children's Bureau, 8 Wakley Street, London EC1V 7QE.
Tel: 020 7843 6000.
Website: www.ncb.org.uk

Registered Charity number 258825.

ISBN 1 904787 26 6

British Library Cataloguing in Publication Data
A catalogue record for this book is available from the British Library

The views expressed in this book are those of the authors and not necessarily those of the National Children's Bureau.

Contents

About the authors   v
Acknowledgements   vii

Introduction   1
  Inclusion and inequalities   3
  About this booklet   4

1 The issues and rationale for promoting inclusion and
    reducing inequalities   7
  The principles underpinning this book   7
  Why promote inclusion and reduce inequalities?   8
  Ensuring effective practice   10
  Addressing inclusion and inequalities through PSHE and
  Citizenship   10

2 The importance of effective policy, participation and
    partnerships   13
  Policy   13
  Participation   13
  Partnerships   14
  An agenda for consultation   16

3 Curriculum development   19
  Planning the curriculum   19
  Step-by-step review   22

Step1a: Identifying the needs of pupils 23
Step1b: Auditing current curriculum provision 24
Step 2: Planning learning outcomes 25
    Key Stage 1 PSHE and Citizenship 25
    Key Stage 2 PSHE and Citizenship 27
    Key Stage 3 PSHE 29
    Key Stage 3 Citizenship 30
    Key Stage 4 PSHE 32
    Key Stage 4 Citizenship 33
Step 3: Deciding the appropriate curriculum context 37
Step 4: Developing schemes of work 37
    Assessment 38
Step 5: Creating a safe and effective learning environment
for children and young people 39
    Classroom ethos 39
    Classroom layout 40
    Valuing experiences 41
    Language 41
    Learning styles 42
    Differentiated learning 44
    Targeting 48
Step 6: Monitoring and evaluating the inclusion curriculum
for personal and social development 48

Endnote 53

Appendix 1: Year plan 55

Appendix 2: Useful resources 57

Appendix 3: Useful organisations 63

Appendix 4: Useful websites for young people 67

References 69

About the authors

Simon Blake is the assistant director of Children's Development at the National Children's Bureau. He is responsible for leading the Personal, Social and Health Education (PSHE) and Citizenship programme of work in education settings. Prior to this, Simon was director of the Sex Education Forum. He is a member of the National Teenage Pregnancy Independent Advisory Group, has written a number of publications on all aspects of PSHE and Citizenship, and is coeditor of *Spotlight: Promoting emotional and social development.*

Sue Plant is a freelance trainer, writer and consultant. She has extensive experience in PSHE, and a specialist interest in sex and relationships education (SRE) in schools and other educational settings. She has been a teacher, PSHE and Citizenship coordinator, and deputy head of a secondary school.

Sue has worked as a local education authority adviser for PSE with a county-wide responsibility for support and training across all key stages. She has been chair of the Sex Education Forum; a member of the national PSHE Advisory Group; and the chair of the SRE task group on the Teenage Pregnancy in the Department of Health.

Sue has published and contributed to a number of publications including the teachers' notes for the BBC 'Sex Education' series in 1999 for Key Stages 3 and 4; and *PASSPORT: A framework for personal and social development* (with Jane Lees) commissioned by the Calouste Gulbenkian Foundation.

Acknowledgements

We wish to thank Vanessa Cooper, Gill Frances, Lynne Gerlach, Jane Lees and Pam Stoate for commenting on earlier drafts, and Tracey Anderson and Lana Hashem for administrative support. Thank you to Zarine Katrak for the summary of Anti-discriminatory practice on page 8.

We also thank the Calouste Gulbenkian Foundation for funding the development and production of this book and allowing us to reproduce the table in Appendix 1.

Introduction

Inclusion is about everyone having a fair chance.
Young woman, aged 15

Inclusion is at the heart of current children's policy, guidance and practice. This book considers the role of Personal, Social and Health Education (PSHE) and Citizenship in promoting inclusion and reducing inequalities.

Effective inclusion in all aspects of school life is key to achieving the five national outcomes for children that are outlined in *Every Child Matters* (HM Treasury 2003):

- being healthy: enjoying good physical and mental health and living a healthy lifestyle
- staying safe: being protected from harm and neglect and growing up able to look after themselves
- enjoying and achieving: getting the most out of life and developing broad skills for adulthood
- making a positive contribution: to the community and to society and not engaging in anti-social or offending behaviour
- economic well-being: overcoming socio-economic disadvantages to achieve their full potential in life.

The United Nations Convention on the Rights of the Child (1989) also emphasises the importance of inclusion. Article 2 states:

> Parties shall respect and ensure the rights set forth in the present Convention to each child within their jurisdiction without discrimination of any kind, irrespective of the child's or his or her parents' or legal guardian's race, colour, sex, language, religion, political or other opinion, national, ethnic or social origin, property, disability or other status.
>
> Parties shall take appropriate measures to ensure that the child is protected against all forms of discrimination or punishment on the basis of the status, activities, expressed opinions, or beliefs of the child's parents, legal guardians or family members.

There is an evolving commitment, locally, regionally and nationally, to ensure that policies and practices meet the needs of our diverse communities in England. Whether in health, education, the voluntary sector, care or secure settings all of us have a responsibility to ensure that all services for children and young people meet their needs and encourage their full inclusion in society. This means providing positive opportunities and experiences that address any specific inequalities children and young people experience, and also challenging prejudice, discrimination and barriers that prevent inclusion.

In schools, the National Curriculum requires a commitment to inclusion. It secures for all pupils, irrespective of social background, culture, race, gender, differences in ability and disabilities, an entitlement to a number of areas of learning and to develop knowledge, understanding, skills and attitudes necessary for their self-fulfilment and development as active and responsible citizens (DfEE and QCA 1999a and 1999b).

The statutory inclusion statement within the National Curriculum handbooks (DfEE and QCA 1999a and b) describes a school's responsibility to provide a curriculum that meets the specific needs of individuals and groups of pupils. It outlines how teachers can modify, as necessary, the National Curriculum programmes of study to provide all pupils with relevant and appropriately challenging work at each Key Stage. It sets out three principles that are essential to developing a more inclusive curriculum:

1. Setting suitable learning challenges
2. Responding to pupils' diverse learning needs
3. Overcoming potential barriers to learning and assessment for individuals and groups of pupils

In addition, the importance of promoting inclusion and reducing inequalities is increasingly demonstrated in most legislation, government guidance and programmes that are relevant to schools. These include:

- The Healthy Schools Programme (1999)
- Race Relations (Amendment) Act (2000)
- The Disability Discrimination Act (1995)
- Special Educational Needs Code of Practice (2001)
- Choice Protects, Behaviour Education and Support Teams (BEST), based in local education authorities (LEAs)
- Education of Children in Care (SEU 2003)
- *Bullying: Don't suffer in silence* (Smith 2002).

Schools must be safe for learning, playing, developing and growing for all children and young people. Pupils need to feel safe to learn from mistakes and safe to be different. This philosophy lies at the heart of Healthy Schools and is described as a whole-school approach (NHSS 1999). Central to this work is the commitment to developing schools that value diversity; that reflect a commitment to inclusion throughout all school activities; and where all children, young people and their families are able to contribute positively and develop their skills and talents.

Inclusion and inequalities

Inclusion is about doing different things for different people.
Young man, aged 15

I feel included when people look at me right, when they talk about things relevant to me and when I know someone is looking out for me.
Young woman in care, aged 13

Recent guidance from Ofsted emphasises the important role that schools play in promoting educational inclusion (Ofsted 2002). Ofsted describes an inclusive school as a school that attempts to provide equal opportunities for all pupils, whatever their age, gender, ethnicity, attainment and background. It pays particular attention to the needs of, and provision for, different groups of pupils within a school with the aim of improving individual achievements and levels of attainment.

Ofsted develops this further by stating:

> Educational Inclusion is more than a concern about any one group of pupils such as those pupils who have been or are likely to have been excluded. Its scope is broad. It is about equal opportunities for all pupils, whatever their age, gender, ethnicity, attainment and background. It pays particular attention to the provision made for and the achievement of different groups of pupils within a school.

Health inequalities refer to the differences in health experience and health outcomes between different population groups (Department of Health 2002). It recognises that the playing field is not level for all children and young people and that some may experience poorer health outcomes on the basis of a range of issues such as poverty, race and class.

Schools have a clear role to play in promoting inclusion and reducing inequalities through their PSHE and Citizenship curriculum, the whole school ethos and environment, and the pastoral care systems and structures.

About this booklet

This booklet provides advice and support on developing a PSHE and Citizenship curriculum that promotes inclusion through its content and approach.

There are three main sections.

Section 1 offers an exploration of the issues and rationale for promoting inclusion and reducing inequalities.

Section 2 gives a brief summary of the importance of effective policy, participation and partnerships.

Section 3 offers advice and guidance on developing a PSHE and Citizenship curriculum that addresses inequalities and inclusion.

1 The issues and rationale for promoting inclusion and reducing inequalities

The principles underpinning this book

There are four fundamental principles underpinning this book.

1. Children and young people have an entitlement to be taught PSHE and Citizenship in a way that is relevant to them and is underpinned by values promoting equality and respect within the whole school community.

2. Valuing diversity and anti-discriminatory practice (see page 8) must be an integral part of a school's ethos and reflected in all areas of the curriculum. In PSHE and Citizenship, this means the school taking responsibility for consulting and involving partners – including pupils, parents and carers – in the development of policy and practice.

3. Children, young people and their families must be able to work with teachers and school staff to create a safe framework and ethos in which all members of the school community feel able to discuss their views and beliefs. Additional efforts may be needed to help less confident members of the community engage with the process.

4. PSHE and Citizenship is a mainstream entitlement and must also be targeted to meet the needs of marginalised and vulnerable children and young people. As with all subject areas, there must be high expectations for all children and young people.

Anti-discriminatory practice

Anti-discriminatory practice is about how we treat people and how we want to be treated. It is essential in promoting inclusion. Anti-discriminatory practice includes:

- Negotiating and agreeing rules so that everyone signs up to acceptable behaviours.

- Checking out our assumptions about other people's remarks or actions in order to address any misunderstandings before attempting to debate or challenge.

- Being aware that people live in different realities that are equally valid and that they have the right to hold different beliefs and values as long as they do not hurt others.

- Remembering that raising awareness can prevent exclusion in cases where individuals are genuinely ignorant of indirect discrimination experienced by other groups.

- Being explicit that acceptable behaviours in the personal arena may be very different from professional expectations.

- Taking action based on legislation, directives, national and local policies and guidance if individuals and organisations are discriminatory.

Why promote inclusion and reduce inequalities?

It makes me stressed, winds me up, when people bully and tease me.
Young man with a learning disability, aged 19

It is not fair to tease or bully people because they are not like you.
Boy, aged 8

It's what's inside that counts.
Young woman with a learning disability, aged 24

Some children and young people find it hard to actively participate at school and in the community as a result of their life experiences and health inequalities. Those who need additional help and support to fully participate at school may:

- be temporarily or permanently excluded from school
- be infected or affected by HIV
- have learning difficulties, physical disabilities or sensory impairments
- be looked after by a local authority
- be gay, lesbian or bisexual
- be from families with parents or carers who are misusing alcohol or other drugs
- be from lower socio-economic groups
- be experiencing a mental health problem of their own or in their family
- be experiencing violence in the home or community
- be experiencing emotional or behavioural difficulties
- be from minority ethnic communities
- have been, or are being, bullied
- be from a religious group
- be young mothers or fathers
- be experiencing loss as a result of parental separation or divorce, or from bereavement
- be highly mobile, for example Travellers, refugees or asylum seekers.

Recent national policy has stressed the importance of robust systems and structures, and working to standards of best practice. Increasingly, evidence from research and best practice tells us this alone is not enough. Having the opportunity to develop significant relationships with one or two adults is also very important for vulnerable children and young people.

For too long, initial teacher training and INSET has focused on the knowledge needed to deliver the National Curriculum, with its emphasis on standards and achievement. The non-statutory nature of PSHE (across the Key Stages) and Citizenship (Key Stages 1 and 2) has meant that it has occupied a relatively weak position within the school curriculum and has, as a result, seen only limited professional development. Consequently there is an overall lack of confidence with the content and participatory methodology of PSHE and Citizenship, which makes it difficult to develop more targeted and inclusive practices. Everyone who works with children and young people needs to receive initial training and continued professional development to enable them to develop and sustain emotionally competent and caring relationships with children and young people (Batmanghelidjh 2004).

Ensuring effective practice

Schools can effectively address the needs of all children and young people by:

- ensuring that mainstream entitlement of PSHE and Citizenship for all children and young people explicitly addresses inequalities, diversity and inclusion issues
- ensuring there is targeted provision whereby children and young people who require extra support receive it, both within the school and through services in the wider community
- ensuring there is access to pastoral support in school and in the wider community, so that children and young people can receive one-to-one support and, where necessary, be supported through effective referrals
- demonstrating a commitment to valuing diversity and helping children and young people to respect difference.

Addressing inclusion and inequalities through PSHE and Citizenship

The government is demonstrating its commitment to promoting the emotional and social development of children and young people through:
- the publication of the first ever Frameworks for PSHE and Citizenship, published in the National Curriculum (DfEE and QCA 1999a and 1999b)

- the development of the Social, Emotional and Behavioural Skills Programme currently being piloted in primary schools across England
- the publication of end of Key Stage statements for PSHE (QCA 2004)
- the Continuing Professional Development (CPD) Strategy of PSHE Certification for teachers (for further information visit www.wiredforhealth.gov.uk).

Inclusion can be promoted as part of the personal and social development of children and young people through the PSHE and Citizenship curriculum and off-timetable opportunities. Additional pastoral support and guidance may be needed by some pupils temporarily, such as when bereavement occurs. Some may need longer term support, not only while the child or young person is at school but beyond that into adult life. Effective PSHE and Citizenship is particularly important in helping vulnerable children and young people to develop a secure sense of identity and to function well in the world (Blake and Muttock 2004).

Work that supports personal and social development is key to promoting inclusion through: the exploration of different cultures and stereotypes; developing empathy and understanding; and developing the skills and confidence to interact with people who are different. It provides an opportunity to ensure that discussions of difference and diversity are fostered and encouraged in a safe and positive way, and that children and young people recognise that 'being different is normal'. It supports inclusion by helping children and young people to develop the understanding, confidence and skills to:

- understand themselves, and use their emotions and thinking skills together
- identify and challenge their own stereotypes and those of others
- understand and value difference and diversity
- manage and deal with prejudice and discrimination, and ask for help where necessary
- empathise with and support people who experience prejudice and discrimination

- understand how prejudice and discrimination create and exacerbate social and health inequalities
- look after their own health and promote the health and well-being of others
- claim their own rights, manage their responsibilities and respect the rights of others
- interact with and respect the rights of people who are different from themselves
- make sense of their life experiences and the experience of others and use them to inform future decisions
- develop healthier lifestyles and discuss health issues with families and the community.

2 The importance of effective policy, participation and partnerships

Policy

The process of developing a PSHE and Citizenship policy is as important as actually having a policy. The policy will most effectively support best practice if it explicitly addresses:

- how inclusion can be assured
- how the school identifies any pupils with additional education and support needs
- how pupils' additional needs will be addressed, for example through learning mentor support.

The development process must also be inclusive and actively provide consultation opportunities for all members of the school community to contribute, including young people themselves. Additional efforts may be needed to secure the participation of vulnerable children, young people and their families, but they need to know that they have an important role in ensuring that their needs are met.

Participation

Children and young people have the right to participate in all issues that affect them (Article 12 UNCRC, 1989). Evidence suggests that the experience of participating may have a particularly beneficial impact on those who are vulnerable (Madge and others 2004).

The Department for Education and Skills has produced guidance, *Working Together: Giving pupils a say* (DfES 2004), to support schools and local education authorities to enable pupil participation. Complementary guidance has been published by the Healthy Schools Programme (Health Development Agency 2004).

Active steps may need to be taken to ensure that those who feel excluded or who are vulnerable feel able to participate. Creative approaches such as drama, music, rap and poetry have all proven to be useful ways of eliciting the views and ideas of vulnerable and marginalised young people. As one young man who used poetry as a way of expressing himself said, 'It's easier to say what I mean on paper, no one has to look at me and I can say what I really feel.'

Partnerships

Partnerships – including those with children and young people, their families and a wide range of community partners – really help move work forward. Partnerships with parents and carers, especially those of children and young people most vulnerable to exclusion, are vital to developing effective PSHE and Citizenship.

Schools need to have the confidence of parents and carers in the community they serve. The government is actively encouraging schools to consult parents and carers when they develop PSHE and Citizenship. The need for consultation is emphasised in the DfEE's *Sex and Relationship Education Guidance* (2000) and the Healthy School's Guidance (1999). Ofsted inspections require schools 'to inform parents and carers fully in providing for the particular needs of their children' and will ask for comments to this end in the pre-inspection questionnaire. They will also ask parents, carers and pupils specifically about bullying.

The issues parents, carers and the community will be interested in will vary depending on the local community. Examples of issues schools have addressed include:

- finding solutions to enable Asian girls to participate in sport
- enabling the observance of religious customs and practices
- helping Traveller parents to maintain continuity in the education of their children
- supporting families where children have long-term illnesses or are young carers
- addressing the concerns of parents and carers with children who are gifted or talented, or who have learning difficulties
- supporting children and young people with behavioural problems so that they can achieve and allow others to learn
- ensuring asylum seekers and refugees are supported to access the curriculum when they first begin school in England
- reviewing their curriculum work on sex and relationships to ensure that the work includes the spectrum of beliefs and views on different issues.

In order to communicate effectively with parents and carers, a school may have to consider:

- providing translations of school letters and documents
- communicating individually with those whose literacy skills are limited
- actively engaging those who may find it difficult to approach school
- working to resolve conflicts between different ethnic groups in its community
- learning about its parental community, so as to use its strengths to support pupils' learning
- holding meetings at appropriate times and in single sex groupings.

Involving parents, carers and the local community in the identification of needs and curriculum planning develops their confidence that all pupils are receiving equity of provision in PSHE and Citizenship and that specific needs are being met. It also increases the likelihood of parents and carers reinforcing the learning at home.

Consultation can be carried out through:

- questionnaires given out at parents' meetings, or while they wait for appointments
- questionnaires sent home
- inviting a group of parents representing each year group to meet with the PSHE coordinator
- inviting to an informal meeting those parents who find it hard to come to school
- meeting with community representatives.

An agenda for consultation

The content of the questionnaires or the agenda for discussion, specific to PSHE and Citizenship, can be drawn from the framework of Learning Outcomes for Inclusion (page 25).

Once the curriculum for PSHE and Citizenship is completed, it is good practice to:

- send a summary of the policy to parents and carers
- put an outline programme for each year group in the school prospectus, making the full policy available on request
- call a meeting at the start of each Key Stage to explain the programme to parents and carers and to show them some of the activities and resources used.

In some areas of PSHE and Citizenship, such as sex and relationships education, parents and carers from minority cultural and faith groups may need additional reassurance that their values and beliefs will be respected. Evidence suggests that misunderstandings about the content of sex and relationships education exacerbate mistrust and hostility (Blake and Katrak 2002). Parents tend to feel more confident when they understand that their beliefs and values will be respected and that sex and relationships education is about helping children and young people to understand themselves; to feel good about their changing bodies and relationships; to develop the skills of being able to make and keep relationships and keep themselves safe; and to understand the concepts of responsibility and respect.

When working with families who have strong cultural beliefs and values, such as Traveller families, schools may need to work with support groups and offer opportunities for some aspects of PSHE and Citizenship to be delivered at home in order to maintain continuity in children and young people's education (Evans 2004).

Communication with the carers of looked after children will be necessary to meet the statutory rights of children in care. Partnerships with the parents and carers of children and young people with a learning disability are vitally important to ensure reinforcement of the learning and consistency of approach. The fpa has produced two resources which schools can encourage parents and carers to use (Kerr-Edwards and Scott 2001 and 2003) (see Useful resources).

Partnerships with learning mentors, Connexion personal advisors and community organisations will provide opportunities to access expertise in both planning and delivery, for example when working with refugees and asylum seekers.

3 Curriculum development

Planning the curriculum

Research suggests there is a range of core emotional and social qualities that can be nurtured to promote inclusion and reduce inequalities. These include:

■ supporting children and young people to develop empathy with others
■ developing a positive sense of self
■ recognising how emotions impact on decision-making and beliefs
■ developing an understanding of rights and responsibilities
■ developing an acceptance of diversity and difference
■ developing participation and active citizenship skills.

(Calouste Gulbenkian Foundation 1998, National Healthy School Standard 2003b)

These skills and qualities can be developed through PSHE and Citizenship. If done well, PSHE and Citizenship help children and young people to develop a secure sense of identity and to function well in the world. It includes three elements that support inclusion:

■ the acquisition of accessible, relevant and age-appropriate information
■ the clarification and development of attitudes and values that support self-esteem and are positive to health and well-being

Figure 1: A combined delivery model for PSHE and Citizenship (with relevance to Inclusion)

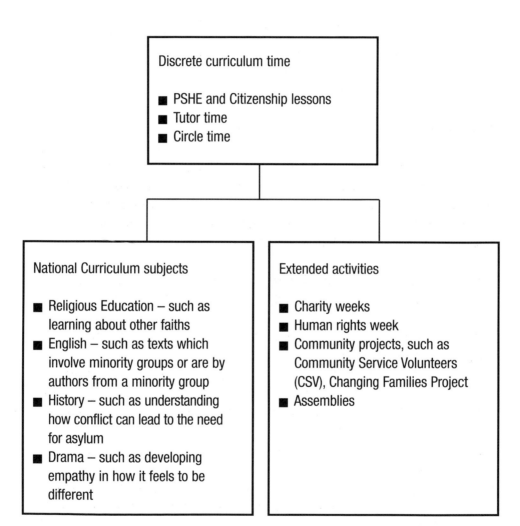

■ the development of personal and social skills to promote:
  - emotional development and interaction with others
  - positive health choices
  - active participation in society and access to support services.
(NCB 2003)

PSHE and Citizenship provide a curriculum focus for children and young people to acquire knowledge about health and well-being; develop life skills, including emotional literacy; and explore and develop attitudes and values that support positive self-esteem and confidence. It also enables children and young people to learn about and value diversity, both in school and in the wider community.

The frameworks for PSHE and Citizenship (DfEE and QCA 1999a and 1999b) are important vehicles through which schools can make explicit their planned provision for pupils' personal and social development. PSHE and Citizenship involves a whole curriculum approach and can be found in any National Curriculum subjects, in planned opportunities outside the National Curriculum subjects, and as discrete PSHE and Citizenship lessons, as demonstrated in Figure 1.

The following points identify the rationale for, and advantages of, addressing inequalities and inclusion in PSHE and Citizenship.

■ It enables teachers and pupils to respond to the diverse learning needs of the learners.
■ It provides a curriculum context for pupils to learn to recognise stereotypes, bullying and racial harassment situations, and develop skills to challenge these behaviours and to resolve conflicts that may arise as a result of difference.
■ It makes use of, and celebrates the range of, social and cultural backgrounds within the school and its wider community.
■ It encourages research into the demographic profiles of the various communities that make up today's United Kingdom society, whether or not the school has a diverse community.
■ It provides a context for all pupils, whatever their differences, to be given opportunities to relate their stories and become valued members of their school communities.

- It encourages staff and pupils to work together to overcome barriers to learning.
- It promotes the involvement and participation of all pupils, and encourages those who may not normally participate to do so.
- It helps the development of positive relationships with local, national and global communities.
- It ensures effective links to confidential advice offered with in the school and in the community, and ensures timely and supported referrals.

Step-by-step review

PASSPORT: A framework for personal and social development (Lees and Plant 2000), which informed the development of the PSHE and Citizenship Frameworks in the National Curriculum, details a step-by-step process of analysing needs, auditing current practice and planning programmes. The principles are supported and developed by subsequent documentation from the Qualification and Curriculum Authority and the National Healthy School Standard.

The following are steps that individual schools can helpfully take when reviewing and adapting the PSHE and Citizenship curriculum to ensure, in particular, that inequalities and inclusion issues are addressed:

1a Identify the needs of pupils who are at risk of exclusion and inequalities, and the needs of others in order to promote better understanding and awareness of diversity and prejudice.
1b Audit the current whole curriculum provision.
2 Plan appropriate learning outcomes.
3 Decide which is the appropriate curriculum context.
4 Develop schemes of work, including one for assessment.
5 Create a safe and effective learning environment for children and young people.
6 Monitor and evaluate the inclusion curriculum for personal and social development.

Step 1a: Identifying the needs of pupils

Ofsted states that to be educationally inclusive, schools 'need to be vigilant in identifying pupils' individual needs and monitoring their progress'. As part of the self-evaluation and inspection process, schools are required to identify if pupils are vulnerable, experiencing inequalities, or at risk of social or educational exclusion. This process will result in an understanding of the diversity of the school community.

Example from Ofsted 'Evaluating Educational Inclusion' (2000) – Extract from report on a primary school

Information about the school: Smithville Infants School serves a small, well-established council housing estate in the heart of England; its 175 pupils live on the estate. Most classes have an equal number of boys and girls and the school population is predominantly white. About a quarter of the pupils are on the Special Needs Register. Four pupils have Statements of Special Educational Need and this is average for schools of this type. The number of pupils eligible for free school meals is well above average for infants schools. The school is involved in a Family Learning programme for literacy.

The next step is to identify the particular learning needs of children and young people to ensure each pupil's full access to a broad and balanced curriculum. A number of issues may need to be addressed, for example those of:

- using appropriate language
- ensuring that the needs of pupils with physical disabilities and sensory impairments are catered for, such as space for wheelchairs, aids for those with hearing or visual impairments
- managing the cultural and faith issues which might prevent pupils taking part
- providing appropriate challenges, including for the gifted and talented
- providing an environment which assumes children, young people and their families will have a range of sexualities, life experiences and histories

- providing support for young people who might be at risk and/or need support, for instance pregnant teenagers, young carers, sick pupils and pupils with challenging behaviour
- recognising some children, young people and their families may be living with HIV (see Lewis 2001)
- ensuring relevant preparatory and follow-up work is planned for pupils with special educational needs
- using resources that are representative and inclusive of different cultures, ethnicities and disabilities
- actively supporting bereaved children and young people by planning with them and their families the implementation of individual support plans.

The DfES, QCA and NHSS all recommend that any needs analysis, in relation to PSHE and Citizenship, should be based on self-identified pupil needs and supported by: the views of others who know them, for example parents, carers, health professionals, and teachers; and data, such as local teenage pregnancy rates, attendance records, exclusion data and bullying records. Children and young people can be involved in carrying out surveys of their peers.

The needs analysis process will also pinpoint specific topic areas that should be included in the curriculum, for example stereotyping, understanding disability or prejudice relating to culture or sexuality. Thus, support will be offered, and awareness, understanding and respect for individuals and groups who are different will be developed.

Step 1b: Auditing current curriculum provision

Having identified the needs, an audit of the existing curriculum will:

- highlight gaps in provision
- show whether the needs of different pupils are planned for and addressed
- show whether any topic areas need to be developed to contribute to promoting inclusion.

As PSHE and Citizenship is delivered across the whole curriculum, the PSHE and Citizenship lessons, National Curriculum subjects and extended activities should all be included in the auditing process.

Step 2: Planning learning outcomes

Once pupils' needs have been identified, it is possible to determine the learning outcomes to meet them. These are expressed in terms of skills, knowledge and understanding, and attitudes and values.

The following framework of learning outcomes is adapted from PSHE and Citizenship and Inclusion (DfES and QCA 1999a) and the PASSPORT learning outcomes. These learning outcomes are a menu not a prescription, and schools should select according to the needs of pupils and the school community identified at Stage 1 of the audit, review and planning process. (These should be used alongside the PASSPORT learning outcomes or the PSHE & Citizenship frameworks.)

Key Stage 1 PSHE and Citizenship

The relevant components of the PSHE and Citizenship framework are as follows.

Developing confidence and responsibility and making the most of their abilities

Pupils should learn:

■ to recognise what is fair and unfair
■ to believe in fairness for all
■ to recognise their uniqueness and feel good about themselves
■ to recognise, name and deal with their feelings in a positive way
■ to develop a sense of self, recognise feelings in themselves and others and to practise thinking and doing whilst acknowledging feelings.

Preparing to play an active role as citizens

Pupils should learn:

- to take part in discussions with one person, who is not a close friend, and the whole class
- to take part in a simple debate about matters relating to their lives, for example bullying
- to recognise the difference between right and wrong
- to agree rules for the classroom and playground
- to know that they belong to different groups and communities, such as family and school
- to support others through activities such as circle time, and to learn to advocate for others through activities such as the school council.

Developing good relationships and respecting the differences between people

Pupils should learn:

- to recognise that their behaviour and words can hurt other people
- to listen to other people, and play and work cooperatively with a range of different people
- to identify and respect the differences and similarities between people, that is in terms of gender, appearance, abilities, families and culture
- to be proud of who they are, and understand that difference does not mean better or worse.

An example at Key Stage 1 – Year 2

A school has an increasing number of families who are asylum seekers with children. A particular need that has been identified is that the children are made to feel welcome and safe. Learning outcomes might be:

■ to talk to someone who is new to this country and find out how their country is different, and what they are proud of about their country
■ to know everyone's names in the class and be able to use them
■ to play with new pupils at playtimes
■ to find out what new pupils need to make them feel good about school.

Key Stage 2 PSHE and Citizenship

The relevant components of the PSHE and Citizenship framework are as follows.

Developing confidence and responsibility and making the most of their abilities

Pupils should learn:

■ to talk and write about their opinions and feelings, and explain their views on issues that affect themselves and society, for example bullying
■ to continue to develop a sense of self and self-esteem, and to recognise and acknowledge the feelings of themselves and others.

Preparing to play an active role as citizens

Pupils should learn:

■ to research, discuss and talk about social issues, for example the diverse range of groups within the school and local community

■ to develop empathy
■ to understand that different groups may have different views and that they are not necessarily wrong
■ to realise the consequences of anti-social and aggressive behaviours, such as bullying and racism, on individuals and communities
■ to value their own identity and background and those of others
■ to resolve differences by looking at alternatives, making decisions and explaining choices
■ to appreciate the range of national, regional, religious and ethnic identities in the United Kingdom
■ to explore how the media present information, for example about disability
■ to support others through peer education, support and to advocate for others.

Developing a healthy, safer lifestyle

Pupils should learn:

■ that pressure to behave in an unacceptable way can come from a variety of sources, including people they know
■ how to ask for help and use basic techniques for resisting pressure to do wrong.

Developing good relationships and respecting the differences between people

Pupils should learn:

■ to care about other people's feelings
■ to think about the lives of people living in the United Kingdom and other countries, and people with different values and customs
■ to realise the nature and consequences of racism, teasing, bullying and aggressive behaviours, and how to respond to them and ask for help

■ to recognise and challenge stereotypes
■ to understand that differences and similarities between people arise from a number of factors, including those of cultural, ethnic, racial and religious diversity; gender; sexuality; and disability.

An example at Key Stage 2

A school is predominantly white and middle-class. A need has been identified to challenge stereotyping of people of African and Asian origin. Learning outcomes might be:

■ to think about the lives of people living in other places and times, and people with different values and customs
■ to think about the lives of Black and Asian friends and families in the United Kingdom
■ to recognise and challenge stereotypes
■ to have a critical understanding of how the media present information about people of African and Asian origin.

Key Stage 3 PSHE

The relevant components of the PSHE framework are as follows.

Developing confidence and responsibility and making the most of their abilities

Pupils should learn:

■ to respect the differences between people as they develop their own sense of identity
■ to feel motivated and value learning.

Developing a healthy, safer lifestyle

Pupils should learn:

■ to recognise when pressure from others threatens their personal safety and well-being, and to develop effective ways of resisting pressures, including knowing when and where to get help.

Developing good relationships and respecting the differences between people

Pupils should learn:

■ to be aware of the effects of all types of stereotyping, prejudice, bullying, racism and discrimination and how to challenge them assertively
■ to empathise with people who are different from themselves
■ to recognise some of the cultural norms in society, including the range of lifestyles and relationships
■ to resist pressure to do wrong
■ to recognise when others need help and how to support them
■ recognise the impact of their actions on others.

Key Stage 3 Citizenship

The relevant components of the Citizenship framework are as follows.

Knowledge and understanding about becoming informed citizens

Pupils should learn:

■ the legal and human rights and responsibilities underpinning society, and how they relate to young people, for example young carers or children with HIV

■ the diversity of national, regional, religious and ethnic identities in the United Kingdom and the need for mutual respect and understanding
■ the importance of resolving conflict fairly.

Developing skills of enquiry and communication

Pupils should learn:

■ to think about topical political, spiritual, moral, social and cultural issues, problems and events – such as prejudice, teenage pregnancy, asylum seekers and refugees, trafficking of children, honour killings – by analysing information and its sources, including internet-based sources
■ to justify orally and in writing a personal opinion about such issues, problems or events, for example the conflict in Iraq and how it affects Muslims and race relations in the United Kingdom.

Developing skills of participation and responsible action

Pupils should learn:

■ to use their imagination to consider other people's experiences and be able to think about, express and explain views that are not their own
■ to negotiate, decide and take part responsibly in both school- and community-based activities that might support excluded young people
■ to support others through peer education and support, and to advocate for others.

An example at Key Stage 3 – Year 9

A school has a unit for physically disabled pupils. Some of the pupils from the unit have reported that they have difficulty in the playground with other pupils bumping into them. Learning outcomes might include:

- to recognise when pressure from others threatens their personal safety and well-being
- to recognise when others need help and how to support them
- to understand how it feels to have a visual impairment, and be able to ask when and how someone with a visual impairment may need support
- to work with disabled children and young people to plan how they will be supported to participate in the school community and activities.

Key Stage 4 PSHE

The relevant components of the PSHE framework are as follows.

Developing confidence and responsibility and making the most of their abilities

Pupils should learn:

- to have a positive sense of their own identity and present themselves confidently in a range of situations
- to consider how the media influence personal opinion about diversity
- to understand how to manage their emotions and recognise how they influence behaviour.

Developing a healthy, safer lifestyle

Pupils should learn:

- to use assertiveness skills to resist unhelpful pressure
- to know the demographic trends in relation to HIV

■ how to look after their health and demonstrate empathy for children, young people and their families living with HIV.

Developing good relationships and respecting the differences between people

Pupils should learn:

■ to understand that there is a diversity of belief and traditions within different ethnic groups
■ to understand the power of prejudice
■ to understand exploitation in relationships
■ to challenge offending behaviour, prejudice, bullying, racism and discrimination assertively and take the initiative in giving and receiving support
■ to challenge personal assumptions about people who are different
■ to work and live with a range of people who are different from themselves
■ to recognise that one can respect people who have different beliefs and lifestyles.

Key Stage 4 Citizenship

The following aspects of the Citizenship programme of study make explicit links with ethnic and cultural diversity, and contribute to the inclusion and equalities agenda as required by the Race Relations (Amendment) Act (2000). They provide broad opportunities for the exploration of difference, exclusion and inclusion, including stigma and prejudice.

Knowledge and understanding about becoming informed citizens

Pupils should learn about:

■ the legal and human rights and responsibilities underpinning society and how they relate to citizens, for example to have a good

understanding of the range of people who might be disadvantaged both locally and globally
■ the origins and implications of the diverse national, regional, religious and ethnic identities in the United Kingdom and the need for mutual respect and understanding
■ the United Kingdom's relations in Europe, including with the European Union, and relations with the Commonwealth and the United Nations, as they relate to immigration and asylum seeking.

Developing skills of enquiry and communication

Pupils should learn how to:

■ research a topical political, spiritual, moral, social or cultural issue, problem or event – such as immigration laws, or physical and emotional abuse – by analysing information from different sources, including the internet and other computer-based sources, showing an awareness of the use and abuse of statistics
■ express, justify and defend orally and in writing a personal opinion about the above issues, problems or events
■ contribute to group and exploratory class discussions, and take part in formal debates, for example around issues of diversity.

Developing skills of participation and responsible action

Pupils should be taught to:

■ use their imagination to consider other people's experiences and be able to think about, express, explain and critically evaluate views that are not their own, for example to consider what it might be like to be a child of a newly arrived immigrant family
■ negotiate and take part responsibly in school- and community-based activities
■ support others through peer education and support, and to advocate for others.

Example at Key Stage 4

Through monitoring bullying incidents, a school has discovered that homophobic language and abuse is rife in the playground and a number of pupils have reported name-calling. The learning outcomes might be:

■ to challenge personal assumptions about people who have different sexualities
■ to understand the impact of prejudice
■ to learn to respect the rights of others to have different beliefs and live different lifestyles
■ to use their imagination to consider other people's experiences and be able to think about, express and explain views that are not their own, especially in a range of lifestyles and relationships
■ to understand the development of policy and practice designed to reduce homophobic bullying.

The 'Breadth of opportunities' section of the PSHE and Citizenship Frameworks provides opportunities for active participation in activities that help promote inclusion and reduce inequalities. There is a range of opportunities available where pupils:

■ act as a befriender (or mentor), for example for a peer with a physical or sensory disability, or as a playground mediator where arguments develop over differences
■ gain recognition for leading and participating in anti-bullying initiatives and evaluating them, for example through the Diana, Princess of Wales Memorial Award for Young People (see Useful organisations)
■ work with people from the local, national and global community, including community and religious leaders and national and international aid organisations
■ communicate with children in other countries by web-conferencing, email or letters
■ demonstrate respect and understanding between different minority groups within the school and local community and deal with harassment

- contribute to the development, implementation, review and monitoring of school policies about anti-bullying or equal opportunities
- work together in a range of groups and social settings with peers and others, exploring and discussing issues such as the similarities in and differences between cultures, races and religions; how it feels not to be able to see/hear/walk; what being a young carer involves
- provide peer information and advice services
- develop and implement strategies to challenge discrimination when they experience or observe it
- participate in community activities, for example visiting the local elderly people's home, fundraising for a local voluntary organisation.

Case study: Eastbury Comprehensive School, Barking, London

Sixth formers at Eastbury Comprehensive School have teamed up with Age Concern to put on a weekly programme of fun activities for elderly members of the local community, with the help of the charity Community Service Volunteers.

Each Wednesday afternoon, elderly residents are invited into Eastbury's brand new sixth form centre, and are offered the opportunity to play a variety of popular board games with the young people and assist them with art activities. The elderly residents are also taught how to use a computer and use the internet on Eastbury's new, state-of-the-art IT suite.

The project has now been running extremely successfully for over a year. Each week up to 30 local elderly residents come to the centre to meet the young people. The school's sixth formers – who came up with the idea – are totally responsible for organising and running the project, which includes organising the refreshments, initiating and running activities, and welcoming and socialising with the visitors.

The project is seen as an enjoyable and interactive way of bringing together different generations, and is vital in strengthening the bonds between the young and elderly communities in and around Barking. By being involved with the project, young people have seen an increase in their own self-confidence, communication and organisational skills, and a heightened understanding and empathy with the everyday issues faced by senior citizens.

Step 3: Deciding the appropriate curriculum context

Once the learning outcomes have been determined, schools can decide the most appropriate curriculum context in which to address issues and complete the planning process.

For example, after reading a text in English about a minority ethnic group represented in the class or school, pupils can discuss how it feels to belong to that culture, so furthering their understanding of diversity. Where this work takes place in subjects other than PSHE and Citizenship, learning outcomes for PSHE and Citizenship will need to be written into and explicitly identified in the scheme of work for English, and used as basis for assessing and reporting on personal and social development.

Where pupils have a personal education plan or identified personal and social development goals, any groupwork or targeted individual work that contributes to these goals must be identified and reported on.

Step 4: Developing schemes of work

As with other subjects, schemes of work should be written for PSHE and Citizenship. Using the year plan (Appendix 1, page 55), the final column will indicate which department is responsible for the particular learning outcomes. These need to be built into existing schemes of work. For discrete PSHE and Citizenship lessons, the documentation should include:

■ aims
■ learning outcomes
■ resources
■ teaching methodology
■ planning for differentiation (see below)
■ opportunities for assessment.

The QCA schemes of work for Citizenship contain units of work which are specific to diversity. Examples of these include: in Key Stages 1 and 2, Unit 5, *Living in a Diverse World*, and Unit 7, *Human Rights*; in Key Stage 3, Unit 4, *Britain – a diverse society*; and Key Stage 4, Unit 3, *Challenging racism and discrimination*. These are useful materials for developing an understanding of diversity. As well as planning schemes of work, PSHE and Citizenship can respond to contemporary events as they arise in the wider society or in response to incidents that happen within the school.

For example in November 2003, a caravan painted with pictures of a Gypsy family fronted a chanting procession through Lewes in East Sussex. The caravan was set alight as part of a Guy Fawkes event to protest the issues and concerns about Traveller communities in the local area. This was reported in the national press and provided a real-life opportunity to explore prejudice and stereotypes of Traveller families.

Opportunities continually arise through activities reported in the press, for example British Nationalist Party activity and test cases in the High Court or European Court of Human Rights.

Assessment

The purposes of assessment are to highlight what the children and young people have learned, to help teachers and their groups plan what they need next and to inform parents of their children's progress. The identified learning outcomes provide a focus for assessment of learning. These will include elements of skills, knowledge and understanding, and attitudes and values.

Where a relevant topic is delivered through another National Curriculum subject or other opportunity, the subject scheme of work or project should make references to learning outcomes for PSHE and Citizenship, including inclusion, and contain inbuilt opportunities for assessment. The process of pupil assessment in discrete PSHE and Citizenship lessons also needs to be built into schemes of work.

Assessment should be grounded in self-assessment by the children and young people so that they can be involved in their learning and planning. However, the process of self-assessment needs to be supported and validated by other information. This can come from teachers, peers or other adults; from tests and written work; or from certificates that show that a young person has taken part in a community venture, been a mentor or a buddy to someone who needs support. Other sources of evidence can come from role-play, video/audio material, diaries, observation, display or one-to-one reflection.

Further help can be obtained from the QCA's *Citizenship at Key Stages 1–4 Guidance on assessment, recording and reporting* (2002). This is a useful guide for assessing, recording and reporting learning across PSHE and Citizenship.

Step 5: Creating a safe and effective learning environment for children and young people

Creating a safe environment is crucial in enabling children and young people to participate fully in the learning process. This section offers guidance on effective strategies for creating a safe environment for learning.

Classroom ethos

The classroom ethos must be one in which every person feels safe, confident and valued. This is vital for positive self-esteem, and to encourage a positive view of difference. Welcoming children and parents by name into the school and classroom is greatly valued. Every staff member should provide a positive role model of inclusive behaviour, and should maintain pupil dignity even when challenging a pupil's behaviour. One strategy is to have ground rules for the classroom and the playground. The pupils will adhere better to a set of rules that they themselves have drawn up than to a set presented to them.

Typically, agreements that enable inclusion in the classroom would include the need:

■ to value everybody's contribution
■ to allow everyone to have a turn
■ to respect different points of view
■ to understand that we are all unique
■ to try not to use offensive language, stereotyping and prejudice
■ to ask questions if they do not understand
■ to be able to pass or to leave the group if they wish, without comment.

Rules for the playground might include:

■ to help those who need it, for example those who are new to the school and do not have any friends, those who have recently been bereaved, visually impaired pupils
■ to include everyone in games and activities
■ to report any instances of bullying including name-calling.

These rules and agreements need to be reviewed from time to time to see whether they are still appropriate and whether they are being adhered to.

Classroom layout

The classroom's layout can support or inhibit effective learning. Placing chairs in a circle so everyone can see and hear each other demonstrates equality and respect. Resources need to be placed at an appropriate level and marked with labels or pictures to facilitate access for all pupils. Space is needed for wheelchair users so that they can move freely and become independent learners. Pupils with auditory impairments should be seated in a position where they can best hear, with the teacher constantly aware of where they are in the room. Pupils with visual impairments will be most secure if the classroom layout and resources do not constantly change so that they know where they are, and so that they, too, can access resources. If there is space, a respite or quiet area can provide a space for children who need time out to calm down or opt out without losing face.

Valuing experiences

Children and young people thrive in a climate that values the individual and their experiences. Class displays that reflect and celebrate difference and diversity, and that include the use of community languages, support such a climate. Many primary schools have a system of 'Today's special person' where every child in a class is the focus of attention for one or more days over the course of an academic year. The special person is given privileges such as receiving more positive feedback than usual, especially from their peers, and going into dinner first.

Case study: St David's Church of England First School, Exeter

The whole school (including administrative staff and learning support assistants) attend daily collective worship, although any child or adult has the right not to participate. Collective worship follows a weekly pattern. On Fridays, the whole school will celebrate the achievements of a special person. This may recognise the special qualities of one particular child or allow other celebratory opportunities, such as presentation of the Lunchtime Play Leaders' Award for a child who has been most consistent in using the words 'please and thank you' during the week.

Language

Culturally sensitive, non-patronising and non-assuming language i̶n̶ classroom and the school community fosters a sense of inclus̶i̶ It is important not to develop and perpetuate a 'them and u̶ syndrome. Using questioning techniques and language̶ discussion and understanding of difference, rather t̶ of 'what is normal' promotes an inclusive envir̶ using 'parents and carers' rather than 'pare̶ after children. Language around sexuali̶ children, young people or member̶

In primary schools, there are some children who are living with two parents and carers of the same gender. Research has shown that children as young as seven or eight know that they feel different but do not understand why their needs are ignored. In secondary schools, there will a number of young people who are struggling with their sexual identity as they go through adolescence, and there will be others who have a clear sense of their own sexual identity, some of whom will be gay, lesbian or bisexual. Discussion about Traveller communities and faith groups should not assume homogeneity amongst the different cultural communities.

It is important to use language that shows you understand that some children and young people have been bereaved or experienced the divorce or separation of their parents.

Learning styles

Children and young people learn in different ways, and lesson planning will need to take into account the learning styles of the range of pupils in the class. Including a range which allows those who learn in different ways 'n' (kinaesthetic), visual or auditory met les of learning.

'ting and analysing) is the rsonal, social and 'ren and young people hing, support positive s include discussion, nd collaborative rstanding of how opment. Effective oung people to between people ort each other. le to develop and values.

Figure 2: The experiential learning cycle

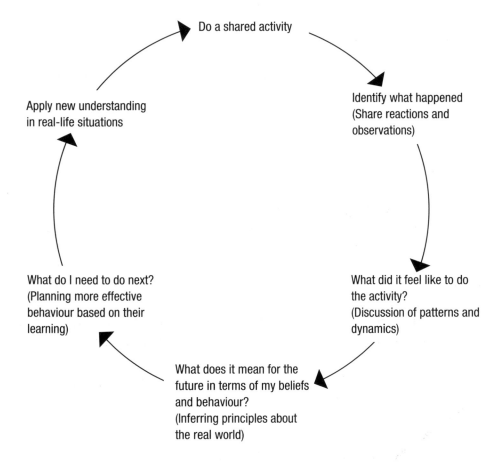

Adapted from *1983 Annual Group Facilitators Handbook* (edited by Jones and Pfeiffer)

The most important aspect of experiential learning is the reflective process, both during and at the end of the activities, as this ensures that learning becomes concrete and helps children and young people to move from concept to action. Figure 2 builds on Kolb's experiential learning cycle.

Play and creative approaches such as art, drama, dance, film-making, sculpture and literature are particularly helpful in providing opportunities for vulnerable children and young people and those with low literacy levels to express their views and ideas. Further information about play and creative approaches is available in 'Play, Creativity and Emotional and Social Development' (Cooper and Blake 2004)

Helpful reflective questions include:

■ What did I do?
■ How did I feel during the process?
■ What did I learn to do and what did I learn about?
■ How can I use this learning in the future?
■ What might help and hinder me in using the learning?

Questioning skills can take account of ability and disposition. For children and young people who have a limited understanding of English, or those with additional learning needs, questions may need to be short and simple, and sometimes closed (with a 'Yes' or 'No' answer), while more complex and open questioning will challenge the more able.

Differentiated learning

Planning for differentiation will ensure that the different needs of children and young people are catered for in any one classroom. Differentiation can be by group, outcome, task or resources.

Groups

The grouping of the pupils in lessons is very important – teachers should pay attention to whether groups are 'fit for purpose'. As far as possible pupils should be mixed in relation to ethnicity and culture, as there is valuable learning to be gained from each other.

Occasionally, pupils may need to be separated by gender. For example, within Sex and Relationship Education programmes, some parents and carers may only allow their children to take part if they have separate lessons. Also, some children and young people report that discussion about particular aspects of sex and relationships is often more fruitful if boys and girls are separated, either within groups in the classroom or in separate classes.

In one school, Year 9 boys who were separated from the girls for a 10-week unit on sex and relationships reported that they were much more able to talk confidently about themselves as the girls considered them childish. When they returned to their mixed-gender groups the girls noted a change in the maturity of the boys in discussions. Year 6 pupils generally prefer to be taught about puberty together and to learn about puberty for both boys and girls. But both girls and boys generally like to have a 'separate session' as well, to have their specific questions answered.

At times it may be helpful to group pupils according to ability or social behaviour, so that a classroom assistant or peer mentor can be assigned to support particular groups.

Outcome

In a truly inclusive society individuals will be able to work with others who are different from themselves. Therefore, as far as possible, pairs and groups should be mixed in terms of ability. The same task is given to all pupils, but teachers have different expectations of different pupils. It is part of each pupil's responsibility to develop the task as far as their ability enables them to. For those who achieve the task satisfactorily, providing extension tasks will deepen their learning.

Task

Whatever the range of differences within the groups, the tasks planned must meet the needs of each child. They might necessitate groups of 'like' pupils – the following examples are provided.

In a group of Year 8 pupils learning about the effects of drug misuse, having watched a knowledge-based video, pupils with learning disabilities could be given a simple quiz to do with a partner in order to check what they have learned. Pupils with English as an additional language could be given picture cards to match to the drug and be asked to draw the effects. The most able pupils may be asked to research independently, and to prepare a joint presentation focusing on substance misuse.

When exploring different lifestyles, pupils with similar backgrounds could be asked to prepare presentations about their lifestyle around a specific topic, for example families or marriage.

Activities which involve writing at the end of a lesson or a unit, in order to record learning, can be varied according to need – from 'cloze' procedure for pupils who have learning difficulties (filling in the words) to more open-ended critical and analytical writing for the more able. A classroom assistant can work with able pupils who have limited language abilities.

Resources

Published educational texts, videos, pictures and posters are now much better than they were in representing the positive images of differences and reducing stereotyping, but they still need to be carefully checked. Are there pictures of children and young people with disabilities? Are there positive images of different cultures? Is the language inclusive? The following is a useful checklist for considering which resources to use and any adaptations that may be necessary.

- Is it consistent with the school ethos and mission statement?
- Is it appropriate to the needs of your children and young people in terms of language, images, attitude, maturity, understanding and the knowledge required?
- Is it explicit enough to meet the needs of all pupils?
- Does it encourage discussion of, and respect for, difference and diversity and avoid racism, sexism, gender and homophobic stereotyping?

■ Does it exclude any young people on the basis of home circumstance, gender, race, literacy, culture, disability, faith or religion?

■ Does it include positive visual images of a range of children, young people and their family circumstances and life experiences?

■ Can it be used as trigger material for discussions of difference or exclusiveness, prejudice and stigma?

■ Can the resource be adapted for use with particular groups of children and young people?

■ In video and multimedia resources, are there images of different children and young people? Will the pupils be able to relate to the visual images, for example the fashions?

■ Is it suitable for children and young people with sensory and auditory impairments: through subtitling, signing or use of large print and Braille?

■ How does it contribute to a broad and balanced PSHE and Citizenship curriculum?

■ Does it encourage active and participatory learning methods?

■ Does it support differentiation?

■ If you have used this resource before, what formal or informal feedback did you receive from children, young people and other workers on it?

■ Does it address assessment of learning and provide opportunities for developing future learning needs?

■ Are you confident about using the resource? What do you need to do to build your confidence in it?

Some children and young people, for instance those who are partially sighted or blind, may need tactile resources such as model genitalia and explicit resources that they can touch and feel. As a group of eight partially sighted young people talking about SRE said, 'We miss out and need information in more detail, more explicit and with models which we can touch.' (HEA and others 2000)

Outside visitors

Visitors to the classroom, or visits to the community, offer an opportunity for positive representation of minority groups in the classroom, and are a way of celebrating and developing an understanding of tolerance and understanding. This may be particularly true where a school community is mono-cultural or living in an area where there are high levels of lone-parent headed households. Many schools celebrate religious and non-religious festivals such as Islamic Eid and the Chinese New Year. Visitors can visit a group or class to talk about their way of life. Preparation for charity events can include researching the needs of the various groups. Whoever the visitors are, they need to be aware of the school's policy on inclusion so that they, like the teachers and other staff in the school, provide positive role models and use appropriate and inclusive resources, language and activities.

Targeting

Classroom assistants provide support for individuals and groups and can be helpful in providing targeted support. For example, where literacy is a problem a classroom assistant can focus on specific groups, explaining and keeping the pupils on task. They can also provide follow-up support outside the classroom, and support children and young people with particular emotional and social development needs. For example, at All Cannings Primary School the special needs coordinator provided a wide range of support both on a one-to-one basis and in small groups, focusing on conflict resolution, behaviour and anger management, and developing the children's ability to use their emotional and thinking skills together.

Step 6: Monitoring and evaluating the inclusion curriculum for personal and social development

Monitoring and evaluation form part of the cycle of the annual school development planning, which is vital to ensuring entitlement to quality learning experiences. The responsibility for monitoring and evaluating the curriculum for personal and social development lies at different levels within a school:

- within classrooms
- with middle managers – subject and pastoral leaders
- with whole-school leadership

■ with the wider school community – parents, governors, and the local community.

Monitoring ensures that the programme is being effectively implemented. It can be carried out by different colleagues using the relevant monitoring questions.

Evaluation is the process that measures whether planned PSHE and Citizenship opportunities are effective and have achieved their aims and objectives, including promoting inclusion and addressing social and health inequalities.

The questions on pages 50–52 can be used as a starting point for monitoring and evaluating provision. Relevant monitoring and evaluation questions for teachers are provided on page 50; for year and Key Stage coordinators on page 51 and for PSHE and Citizenship coordinators on page 52. These can be photocopied and handed out to relevant colleagues.

Monitoring and evaluation questions for classroom teachers

Monitoring questions

- Do tasks engage all pupils actively in their learning and provide pupils with opportunities to work with each other?
- Are resources and tasks differentiated to meet the needs of all pupils?
- Are all pupils given opportunities to reflect on their personal and social learning?
- Is the language used inclusive?
- What feedback have you received from pupils, including those who are vulnerable?
- Is preparatory and follow-up work with identified children and young people being carried out?

Evaluation questions

When evaluating a lesson and a unit of work, ask yourself:

- Have you involved all pupils, including those who are vulnerable, in the evaluation?
- How do you know the lesson aims and learning outcomes about inclusion have been met?
- What went well?
- What will you change next time?

(Adapted from *PASSPORT: A framework for personal and social development*)

Monitoring and evaluation questions for Year and Key Stage coordinators, heads of year, subject coordinators and heads of department

Monitoring questions

■ Do schemes of work identify the core opportunities for ensuring inclusion?
■ How are you monitoring to ensure teaching strategies are inclusive?

Evaluation questions

When evaluating a unit of work which addresses issues around inclusion and inequalities, ask yourself:

■ Have you involved the appropriate people in the evaluation, that is pupils' tutors/subject teachers, other visitors who have contributed to the unit/programme?
■ Have schemes of work sufficiently addressed inclusion?
■ Has sufficient targeted work to support vulnerable children and young people been undertaken, and how has it contributed to the school aims for PSHE and Citizenship?
■ What have been the highlights of PSHE and Citizenship lessons?
■ What targets are needed for development and what actions need to be taken to achieve them?

(Adapted from *PASSPORT: A framework for personal and social development*)

Monitoring and evaluation questions for PSHE and Citizenship coordinators

Monitoring questions

- Do you have procedures for coordinating an inclusion agenda as part of PSHE and Citizenship?
- How are you monitoring the staff involved in the programme at middle management level?
- Is inclusion part of the school development plan?
- Are there any professional development needs being identified?

Evaluation questions

When evaluating the inclusion elements of PSHE and Citizenship as part of the annual review for the school development plan process, ask yourself:

- Have you involved the people representing inequalities as part of the evaluation getting feedback from: pupils; subject and pastoral leaders; parents; outside contributors to the programme?
- Are there sufficient planned opportunities across the curriculum to allow pupils to meet and interact with the community and learn from real-life experiences?
- What has the school achieved over the past year in promoting inclusion as part of PSHE and Citizenship?
- What targets will further develop the inclusion agenda through PSHE and Citizenship?
- What does the action plan imply for staff development and resources?

(Adapted from *PASSPORT: A framework for personal and social development*)

Endnote

Schools need to adopt a holistic and integrated approach to inclusion so that they provide clear and consistent messages. Promoting the personal and social development of all children and young people is the collective responsibility of all staff within schools. PSHE and Citizenship are key curriculum areas for achieving this. However, alone they are not enough, a whole-school approach is needed. As Kochar and Mitchell (2002) state:

> Building an inclusive school is probably one of the biggest challenges facing schools today as they strive to prepare all pupils for life in a complex but stimulating global community. We cannot afford to do otherwise.

As professionals in schools, we have a responsibility to ensure that every single child knows they are important, that we value them and believe in their right to shine. They want to be our partners in making safe and happy school communities in which they can learn, develop and grow.

As one young woman said, 'If I don't feel I am important, why bother to join in.' And, finally, to revisit what one young man told us:

> You have to do different things for different people.

Appendix 1: Year Plan

For curriculum managers, PSHE and Citizenship coordinators

Year...............

Plan the curriculum for personal and social development – inclusion

Priorities for inclusion – identify what pupils should learn

1. Priorities for personal and social development – inclusion	2. Learning outcomes	3. Curriculum context	4. Responsibility
Findings from the needs analysis (Step 1a)	Identify learning outcomes for each priority using the framework of learning outcomes for Inclusion	Select the best opportunity to meet the learning outcomes	Record the member of staff who will be responsible for this part of the curriculum

Adapted from PASSPORT: A framework for personal and social development

Appendix 2
Useful resources

Be Aware: Involving young people in drug policy and practice
National Children's Bureau with the Drug Education Forum (2004)

This package includes a leaflet about drugs and young people's right to participate in policy and practice that has been written and designed by young people. It is accompanied by a briefing on involving young people, and a handbook offering advice on best practice and practical activities for exploring issues relating to alcohol and other drugs with young people.

Childhood Bereavement: Developing the curriculum and pastoral support
Frances, G and Job, N (2004) National Children's Bureau with the Childhood Bereavement Network

Provides guidance and advice for everyone working in and with schools to help children understand and learn about death, bereavement and grief. It also offers practical advice on pastoral care and support for children following bereavement.

Combating Discrimination: Persona dolls in action
Brown, B (2001) Trentham Books

This practical guide to using persona dolls offers a rationale for developing work on prejudice and discrimination and then discusses planning, preparation and use of the dolls.

Developing Sex and Relationships Education in Schools: Guidance and training activities for school governors
Frances, G and Power, P (2003) National Children's Bureau with Sex Education Forum

Provides information about the role and responsibility of school governors in the development of sex and relationships education. It includes background information, training and support activities, and a video.

Doing Different Things for Different People: Children, young people and inclusion
Blake, S and Frances, G (2004) *Spotlight Briefing*

Outlines the key issues and offers advice on promoting inclusion across different settings.

Drugs: Guidance for schools
Department for Education and Skills (2004)

This guidance is based on the principles that underpin good practice in drug education and managing drug incidents.

Index for Inclusion
Centre for Studies of Inclusion (2000)

This set of materials aims to help schools be more inclusive. It provides a systematic way of engaging in school development planning, setting priorities for change, implementing developments and reviewing change.

It's More than Just Listening: Children, young people and participation
National Children's Bureau (2004) National Children's Bureau with Healthy Schools, Peer Support Forum and the Kosh

This 23-minute video with accompanying leaflet offers the direct voices of children and young people talking about participation.

PASSPORT: A framework for personal and social development
Lees, J and Plant, S (2000) Calouste Gulbenkian Foundation

Provides a needs assessment, planning and evaluation tool for teachers to develop curriculum and off-curriculum experiences that meet the needs of pupils.

Promoting Children and Young People's Participation through the National Healthy School Standard
Health Development Agency (2004)

This briefing provides an accessible overview of the theory and practice of actively involving children and young people in school life.

Promoting Race Equality: Policy into practice
Blake, S and Lawrence, P (2003) Optimus Publishing

Offers support for schools and those who work with them to met the legal requirements of the Race Relations (Amendment) Act 2000. It clarifies the legal position and Ofsted's requirements, and offers clear practical advice on developing policy and practice.

PSHE, Citizenship and Traveller Communities
Evans, K (2004) *Spotlight Briefing*, National Children's Bureau

Outlines the key issues and offers ideas and strategies for raising awareness of, and meeting, the needs of Traveller children through PSHE and Citizenship.

Secondary Schools and Sexual Health Services: Forging the links
Thistle, S (2003) National Children's Bureau with Sex Education Forum

Provides guidance for teachers and health professionals on improving young people's access to sexual health services in school and the wider community.

Sex, Alcohol and Other Drugs: Exploring the links in young people's lives
Lynch, J and Blake, S (2004) National Children's Bureau with the Drug Education Forum and the Sex Education Forum

Drawing heavily on the perspectives of young people, professionals and research, this resource brings into the spotlight the links between sexual activity and the use of alcohol and other drugs in young people's lives. It explores young people's opinions about the support they want, and the implications of this for policy and practice. Case studies and practical ideas are used throughout to illustrate how practitioners can address the links between sex, alcohol and other drugs with young people.

Talking Together About Growing Up and Talking Together About Sex and Relationships
Kerr-Edwards, L and Scott, L (2001 and 2003) fpa

These two clearly written books are aimed at parents, teachers and professionals working with young people with learning disabilities. *Talking together about growing up* is designed for work with children aged 8–13; *Talking together about sex and relationships* is aimed at work with young people aged 14 plus. Using pictures and stories, they suggest practical activities for addressing topics such as puberty, independence and assertion skills, friendships, sexual relationships, contraception and sexual health.

Teaching and Learning about HIV: A resource for Key Stages 1 to 4
Blake, S and Power, P (2003) National Children's Bureau with the Sex Education Forum

Provides teachers and others working in primary, secondary and special schools with background information about HIV and activities for use with children and young people, including those with special educational needs.

Teaching and Learning about Volatile Substance Abuse
Blake, S and Butcher, J (2004) *Spotlight Briefing*. National Children's Bureau

Outlines the key issues and offers advice on teaching and learning about volatile substance abuse.

Working Together: Giving children and young people a say
Department for Education and Skills (2004)

This guidance is designed to provide a platform for encouraging best practice for pupil involvement. It reflects comments and suggestions received during the consultation in 2003. The guidance is intended for those involved in providing education services, within local education authorities and schools, as they plan to open up opportunities for children and young people to become more active participants in their education, including involvement in the planning and evaluation of their own learning.

Appendix 3
Useful organisations

Association for Citizenship Teaching (ACT)
020 7367 6510
www.teachingcitizenship.co.uk

Professional subject association for those involved in Citizenship
education. The Association's main aim is the furtherance of mutual
support, knowledge and good practice, skills and resources for the
teaching and learning of Citizenship in schools and colleges.

Diana, Princess of Wales Memorial Award for Young People
ContinYou, 17 Old Ford Road, London E2 9BR
Telephone: 020 8709 9935

The Diana Award helps schools celebrate achievements. It is a non-
competitive award which recognises school students who work as
peer mentors, fund-raisers, young carers, school councillors,
environmental campaigners, sports leaders or those who simply
overcome adversity.

The Award recognises activities already undertaken by pupils – schools
do not need to set up any more systems to qualify.

Drug Education Forum
Mentor UK, 4th Floor, 74 Great Eastern Street, London EC2A 3JG
Telephone: 020 7739 8494
www.drugeducation.org.uk

The Drug Education Forum believes that the purpose of drug education is to increase children's and young people's knowledge and understanding of drugs and their usage, and help them develop skills and attitudes, so that they can make informed choices.

National Children's Bureau
8 Wakley Street,
London
EC1V 7QE
Telephone: 020 7843 6000
www.ncb.org.uk

Offers an information service and produces a range of resources, and offers training and consultancy on all aspects of PSHE and Citizenship.

National Healthy Schools Programme
Health Development Agency, Holborn Gate, 330 High Holborn, London
WC1V 7BA
Telephone: 020 7430 0850
www.wiredforhealth.org.uk

Healthy Schools is a national programme funded by Department for Education and Skills and Department of Health to support schools in becoming healthy schools. Visit the website for contact details.

NSCoPSE
www.nscopse.org.uk

Professional organisation for LEA advisers, inspectors and advisory teachers with responsibility for all aspects of personal and social education, including health education and Citizenship. Membership also includes independent consultants and inspectors, as well as health promotion professionals.

Sex Education Forum
8 Wakley Street, London EC1V 7QE
Telephone: 020 7843 6056
www.ncb.org.uk/sef

The Sex Education Forum is the national authority on sex and relationship education (SRE). It is a unique collaboration of over 50 organisations. The Forum aims to ensure that *all* children and young people receive their entitlement to good quality SRE in a variety of settings. Provides support and information for effective SRE and a telephone information line.

Appendix 4
Useful websites for young people

British Youth Council	www.byc.org.uk
Britkid	www.britkid.org
ChildLine	www.childline.org.uk
Children's Express	www.childrens-express.org
Citizens Connection	www.justdosomething.net/home.vdf
Pupiline	www.pupiline.net
R U Thinking?	www.ruthinking.org.uk
The Site (YouthNet UK)	www.thesite.org
The Who Cares? Trust	www.thewhocarestrust.org.uk
Time for Citizenship	www.timeforcitizenship.com
Trashed	www.trashed.co.uk
Wired for Health	www.wiredforhealth.gov.uk
Wrecked	www.wrecked.co.uk
Young Minds	www.youngminds.org.uk
Youth2Youth	www.youth2youth.co.uk

References

Batmanghelidjh, C (2004) 'Working with vulnerable children and young people: The importance of relationships and loving care', *Spotlight*, 2, 4–6.

Blake, S and Frances, G (2004) 'Doing different things for different people: Children, young people and inclusion', *Spotlight Briefing*, March 2004.

Blake, S and Katrak, Z (2002) *Faith, Values and Sex & Relationships Education*. National Children's Bureau with Sex Education Forum.

Blake, S and Lawrence, P (2003) *Promoting Racial Equality: Policy to practice.* Optimus.

Blake, S and Muttock, S (2004) *PSHE and Citizenship for Children and Young People with Special Needs: An agenda for action*. National Children's Bureau.

Calouste Gulbenkian Foundation (1998) *Learning by Heart: The role of emotional education in raising school achievement.*

Cooper, V and Blake, S (2004) 'Play, creativity and emotional and social development', *Spotlight Briefing*, June 2004.

Department for Education and Employment and QCA (1999a) *The National Curriculum: Handbook for primary teachers in England, Key Stages 1 and 2.*

Department for Education and Employment and QCA (1999b) *The National Curriculum: Handbook for secondary teachers in England, Key Stages 3 and 4.*

Department for Education and Employment (2000) *Sex and Relationship Education Guidance. DfEE.*

Department for Education and Skills (2004) *Working Together: Giving pupils a say.*

Department of Health (2002) *Promoting the Health of Looked After Children.*

Evans, K (2004) 'PSHE and Citizenship and Traveller communities', Spotlight Briefing, August 2004.

Forum on Children and Violence (2001) *A Young People's Charter for Non-violence.*

Hartley-Brewer, E (2002) *Stepping Forward: Working together through peer support*. National Children's Bureau with the Peer Support Forum.

Health Development Agency (2004) *Promoting Children and Young People's Participation through the National Healthy School Standard*.

Health Education Authority, Royal National Institute for the Blind and Sex Education Forum (2000) *Sexual Health Resources for Young People who are Blind or Partially Sighted*. RNIB.

HM Treasury (2003) *Every Child Matters*. The Stationery Office.

Jones, JE and Pfeiffer, JW (eds) (1983) *1983 Annual Group Facilitators Handbook*. John Wiley and Sons.

Kerr-Edwards, L and Scott, L (2001) *Talking Together About Growing Up*. fpa.

Kerr-Edwards, L and Scott, L (2003) *Talking Together About Sex and Relationships*. fpa.

Kerr-Edwards, L (2004) 'Using drama: Sex and Relationships Education for children and young people with disabilities', *Spotlight*, 3, 10.

Kochar, R and Mitchell, L (2002) *Personal and Social Development, Diversity and Inclusion*. NSCoPSE.

Lees, J and Plant, S (2000) *PASSPORT: A framework for personal and social development*. Calouste Gulbenkian Foundation.

Lewis, E (2001) *Afraid to Say: The needs and views of children living with HIV/AIDS.* National Children's Bureau.

Madge, N and others (2004) *National Healthy School Standard and Participation*. Health Development Agency.

National Children's Bureau (2003) *Developing a Whole School Approach to PSHE and Citizenship*.

National Healthy School Standard (1999) *Guidance*. Department of Health and Department for Education and Skills.

National Healthy School Standard (2003a) *Confirming Healthy School Achievement*. Department of Health and Department for Education and Skills.

National Healthy School Standard (2003b) *How the National Healthy School Standard Contributes to School Improvement*. Department of Health and Department for Education and Skills.

National Healthy School Standard (2003c) *Reducing Health Inequalities and Promoting Social Inclusion*. Department of Health and Department for Education and Skills.

Ofsted (2002) *Evaluating Educational Inclusion: Guidance for inspectors*. The Stationery Office.

QCA (2002) *Citizenship at Key Stages 1–4: Guidance on assessment, recording and reporting*.

QCA (2004) *PSHE – End of Key Stage Statements*.

Smith, P (2002) *Bullying: Don't suffer in silence. An anti-bullying pack for schools*. Department for Education and Skills.

Social Exclusion Unit (2003) *A Better Education for Children in Care*. SEU.

United Nations (1989) *The Convention on the Rights of the Child*. Adopted by the General Assembly of the United Nations on 20 November 1989. Geneva: Defence for Children International and the United Nations Children's Fund.